You're Going To Be Great At This!
A Sales Memoir

Chris Castanes

ISBN: 978-1546555162
ISBN-13: 1546555161

DEDICATION

This book is dedicated to sales people, entrepreneurs, business owners and otherwise self-employed, as well as the clients and customers who keep us in business.

CONTENTS

ACKNOWLEDGMENTS

Thanks to all who helped getting this project off the ground, including Mike Oglesbee, who donated his time to teach me the intricacies of self-publishing, my friends at Chastain Media, and of course, my friends and family who encouraged me. Also, I want to extend appreciation to the agents of Surf Financial Brokers (the best sales crew out there!) and our affiliates who have shown unwavering support.

PREFACE

To everyone that sells something, this book is for you. Whether you offer goods or services, we are all selling something. And when you get down to the real root of it all, what you are selling is YOU!

As someone who has been involved in some sort of sales for most of my life, I've endured many books on the subject, along with self-help and motivational books. Most can be quite repetitive and I consider myself fortunate if I can find one or two good pieces of usable material when I take the time to read one.

On the other hand, there just wasn't a book out there (that I've seen) that gives examples of the good, the bad, the horrible, the weird and the great. And sales can be all of that. Hopefully, this is that book.

I started my experiences in sales as a kid. There was always a fundraiser of sorts, either for my church or school or even the YMCA. In the case of the latter, my dad hijacked the box of candy that was assigned to me and urged his staff to make a purchase. Because of this, my basketball team won a trip to see the Harlem Globetrotters at the local arena. I suspected the same happened to all of my teammates and their parents because our team *killed* it.

Walking around our neighborhood and ringing doorbells to raise money was normal for us. Nowadays, it's frowned upon by schools and other organizations. There are too many crazy people out there. But back then, I sold tickets to dinners, packets of seeds, magazine subscriptions and my favorite was Trick or Treating for UNICEF.

Kids have no fear of rejection. That doesn't kick in until you get a little older and insecurities set in. That fear is what separates the successful sales people from the rest of the pack. It keeps us from moving forward, not just in sales, but in every part of our lives.

When I graduated from college, I worked for an insurance company selling accident policies door-to-door. I learned a lot about myself in that short time. I say "short time" because I hated that job and lasted less than a year. From the beginning of the hiring process, my co-workers and I were fed a line of BS that was criminal (we'll go into it later). But I did learn how to sell, cold call, overcome rejection and most importantly, how to move on.

If you know the lay of the land and can see the obstacles before they become problems, fear starts to evaporate. Your job becomes easier and the learning curve smooths out dramatically. That's the goal for this book. I want to share enough to help you get those landmines out of your way ahead of time.

My hope is this. If you or someone you know is seriously considering a career in sales, this book will help you, along with a good personality and good hygiene practices.

As for the title of the book, I stole it from nearly every insurance company's recruiting manager. The truth is that most people don't want to go into a full commission sales job, so the recruiter will blow smoke up your butt and tell you how awesome you are and how easy it is to sell their product. They will also tell you about all of the money you're going to make because, even though they have only known you for four minutes, they know you have a great personality and "you're going to be great at this!"

Keep in mind that *this isn't a motivational book.* It is a book about my experiences that I hope will help you in your career path.

And if you are a customer, client, buyer or consumer, there is something for you as well. We all are on one side or the other during a sale, and if you have a shred of empathy in your soul, you'll relate to something here.

So, with years of experience, humor and perhaps bad taste, I hope to offer some insight into the world of selling.

NOTE: Throughout this book, there are a few "dumb stories" about things I've encountered. They are all true stories and I've changed the names to avoid embarrassing or incriminating anyone. I have tried to clean up the language as much as possible, but I think you'll get the gist. Enjoy!

Chris Castanes

Chapter 1

SELL MUCH?

"The question isn't what are we going to do. The question is what aren't we going to do?" —Ferris Bueller (played by Matthew Broderick) in Ferris Bueller's Day Off

So you are either considering a career in sales or you're already in "the life". Ask yourself a simple question. What am I trying to sell? Is it a car or a subscription to a magazine? Or is it something intangible, like an insurance policy?

Trying to sell any or all of these things has something in common. They are all being sold by other people. There are plenty of folks that are willing to sell me a car, or a magazine or a home. What makes you so special that I should want to spend my hard earned money with you instead of your competitors? And keep in mind that with the internet assisting consumers now, you have even more competitors than you thought.

If you ask your sales manager (I'm not sure that

is always a good thing), he or she may tell you that you have the power of the name of your company behind you. What a load of crap!

Let's return to our original question. What are you selling? Without going into a lot of psychobabble, the answer is that you are selling YOU. (Did you even read the preface?)

Consider this for a moment. You represent XYZ appliances and everyone knows that XYZ makes the best and most reliable appliances ever. Their commercials saturate the airwaves with a recognizable spokesman and a jingle you could sing in your sleep. They are the cream of the crop of appliances.

But you notice that people own all kinds of appliances in their homes, and maybe one is made by XYZ. The rest are okay, but not nearly as good as yours. What gives?

The truth is that the only reason that anyone will buy from you instead of that army of other sales reps is that the buyer likes you. Plain and simple. And you will only get a few seconds to come across as trustworthy, dependable and likeable. That's all it takes these days, but it's vital to your success.

When I was in college, my father and I shopped for a car. We would pull into a lot, get out of our car and a half dozen sales people would walk menacingly toward us like zombies. One would break from the pack and get to us first. Instinctively we became defensive.

During this car buying adventure with my dad, we pulled into a Buick dealership. Because all of the salespeople were tied up with other customers we were free to look around untethered. Then an elderly gentleman walked over to us. I remember him wearing a hat and a cardigan sweater like someone's grandfather in a Norman Rockwell painting. "You fellas looking for anything in particular?" he asked in a very casual manner.

"We're just looking right now," my dad replied. The salesman smiled and nodded.

"Sure, look around. If you need anything I'll be over there." He walked away and didn't bother us while we looked around.

My father looked at a few cars and eventually the old man came over again, gave us his card and said to call him if we had questions. "I bet that guy sells more cars than anyone else on this damn lot," my dad said. And sure enough, the low pressure tactic worked because my dad bought the car a couple of days later.

I kept that old man in my thoughts when I started selling. His calm demeanor and less than pushy technique influenced me. When I look back on all the sales managers I've had who told me I should be more aggressive, I also remember how many of those sales managers are no longer in the business.

Needless to say, I am like many other people who absolutely hate buying a car. I always feel like I just got screwed afterward. Heck, I even had a car salesman lie to me about the content of his company's website and I "must have read it wrong". Thankfully, the internet has made it much easier to get the information on a vehicle like interest rates, trade in values of comparable cars, etc.

I once worked for an insurance company that was very well respected. Our target market was high end professionals, business executives and business owners. Yet when I spoke to these folks they had policies from some of our lesser competitors. When I asked why they purchased from those companies, the response was typically along the lines of, "He was a nice man." Hey, I can be a nice man too!

So my first piece of advice for you is this. *People don't buy from companies; they buy from people they like.* Like I said earlier, it only takes a few seconds for someone to size you up. And if your company is so great, why are they buying from your competitors?

Using empathy, think about how you would react as a customer or a client. We all are trained to put up our guard when someone is selling something. It's natural to be defensive. As professional sales people we need to do our best to knock down that wall as quickly as possible and build a relationship based on trust with the client or customer. Keep in mind that the key to success isn't having the best product, but having the best working relationship with your prospect.

A great way to earn the respect of your client is to sell on their need. We've all heard the expression, "He could sell ice to an Eskimo!" My first response is always, "But did the Eskimo actually need ice?" Seriously, what kind of a jackass would even try to sell ice to an Eskimo?

Listening to your client will help you find a need for your product or service. Ask good questions and continue to drill down on those questions. By "peeling that onion", you will hopefully uncover a need. The prospect will find value in you and your work and you may get more referrals in the long run.

DUMB STORY

After I graduated from NC State (Go Pack!), I interviewed with an insurance company I had never heard of before. I was young and naïve but they promised me the moon and the stars. My big three questions were as follows:

Is there travel involved? What am I getting paid? Where am I supposed to find people to sell to? The recruiter immediately answered all of my questions with things I wanted to hear.

"Yes, there is some travel, but you'll never be more than 30 minutes from your home." In actuality, on my first day in the field, I drove 30 minutes to morning sales meeting, which was followed by another 45 minute haul to where I was assigned to work. Question 1 was answered with a big fat lie.

"You'll be on a commission basis, but if you don't make $20,000 your first year, we'll pay you the difference." Back then $20,000 was decent money. Not the best but decent. He even had a contract that stated in the first paragraph that this was the deal.

As a 23 year old, I didn't read the rest of the contract until much later. It stated that the contract was null and void if I was tardy, disheveled or unprofessional, didn't show an aptitude for the work, etc. and the contract ended the paragraph with the words "or for any other good reason". In a nutshell, the contract wasn't worth the paper it was written on. The answer to question 2 was not a blatant lie, but he wasn't being honest.

Finally, the recruiter answered my final question about getting customers like this.

"We'll give you some customers that already have a policy with us. When you pick up their renewal money, they'll give you names of people to see." What could be better than having satisfied customers handing you referrals?

Of course none of this was true and that is why you see grizzled old insurance agents drinking at a bar at 10am.

In reality, when I called on someone to collect the premium on their existing policy I was supposed to casually ask Mrs. Johnson, "Who lives next door to you?"

"Oh, that's Mr. Porter." *This is not a referral.* It's a name, nothing more.

A few minutes later you are in the driveway next door. Suspiciously, the gentleman comes outside.

"Hello there Mr. Porter!" you state, as if you have met him before. He's taken aback as you go about reintroducing yourself. "I was just talking to Mrs. Johnson and she sent me over here to talk to you." Okay, she didn't, but it did open the door.

So my third question was answered with little regard to the actual way I would be getting prospects. On the whole, I'd have to say the recruiting manager, who was part of a bigger system of lies and misrepresentations, was full of more crap than a Christmas turkey.

It all made me ask myself another question: If this guy was treating me like this, how did he treat his own clients? I'm sure it didn't bother him one bit to "bend this truth" with them as well.

All of this was sneaky and underhanded and was part of our training. As our sales manager would say, "Your income is in their wallets and it's your job to get it out of there." Sweet guy!

Back in my glory days! I often wonder if I could have sold more if I had shaved off this stupid mustache.

Chapter 2

IS SELLING FOR YOU?

*"Right now, this is a job. If I advance any higher, this would be my career. And if this were my career, I'd have to throw myself in front of a train." - **Jim Halpert, The Office***

Before we get into the weeds on this subject, I want to discuss the good and bad of sales from my personal perspective. Not everyone is cut out for this business. There are many people who are better suited to work on a salary because they need that job security. Or they may just be introverted and don't care to get out and meet people, network and create a referral network. Generally, it will take time and a lot of hard work to get started and for many sales people who are independent contractors, it's the same as owning a business.

Selling is tough, especially if for those of us who make our living on a "commission only" basis. It can be lonely, working long hours and away from home. Other times it can seem demeaning. People can just be horrible at times.

On the other hand, if your prospects see the value in what you are offering, they will be happy to meet with you. I've found that the easiest people to sell to are the ones in the same boat I'm in. If you work by appointment as I do, find clients who do the same. They'll be less likely to stand you up and, if they do, most will apologize profusely. (My personal research has shown that apologetic clients buy more often due to guilt.) They realize your time is valuable and will respect that.

I managed a retail store for a few years and as a salaried employee, I was paid the same each week. Great sales or poor sales, my pay didn't change. At times I felt like a glorified babysitter. I'd make sure we had plenty of merchandise in stock, keep payroll down, watch customers to make sure they didn't steal merchandise and if everything was running smoothly, I'd get a pat on the back. But I was restless.

Going above and beyond in that scenario didn't have a great payoff. There was a bonus at the end of the year based off of the store's performance and my evaluation, which was a report my boss wrote. When I divided that annual bonus into weekly segments, it was demotivating.

For example, an annual bonus of $750 meant I had busted my ass for a measly $15 per week!

When I first decided to get into full commissioned sales, there was a lot of anxiety. Then I realized that I could work hard, and that my income wasn't limited to a salary. If I had a great sales week, I could make a lot more money. The key was to keep the poor sales weeks to a minimum. And those bad weeks happened, not just to me but to all of my co-workers.

The tough weeks sucked, but the good weeks made up the difference. And at the end of the year, my income was higher than when I was on a salary. I was also setting my own hours and, more importantly to me, I was doing business with the people I wanted to deal with, and not the ones that I was forced to deal with.

When I was in the retail store, there were rude customers who had been told that "the customer is always right". I had confrontations with shoplifters, drunks, arrogant teenagers and soccer moms who apparently wanted to teach their kids how to treat someone poorly. Now I didn't have to deal with those people anymore.

In the beginning, I have to admit, I was desperate for a client. Your prospects can sense that desperation. We called it "commission breath" because people could smell it on you. And when you have "commission breath" you will take on just about any client on that you can find. Desperation can be a horrible motivator.

With this in mind, I want to quickly cover the three types of business and why people put them in the wrong order.

Good business – These are your best or "A list" clients. On the rare occasion that there is a problem, they understand you're doing your best to fix it. Also, they pay their bill on time and give you referrals. They are awesome!

Bad business – These are folks that take up your time, always have issues and generally are a pain in the ass. The old 80/20 rule comes to mind, which states that 20% of your clients will take up 80% of your time. If you can, you'll want to move that number to 90/10.

No business – This is when you have no one to talk to or nothing in your pipeline. As a salesperson, you'll have to start hustling!

I personally feel that this order or ranking is incorrect. In my world, "no business" is better than "bad business". I'll give you a couple of examples why I think this way.

A few years back, I had a client who wanted five life insurance policies to cover himself, his wife, two kids and a grandchild. And all for under $100 a month! I spent the better part of a day and a half putting together something for this guy and came in at $110. He let me know that it was going to be difficult but he needed some coverage, so he agreed. Then I made two separate trips to his home to get all of the signatures and other information. Two months later all of the policies lapsed.

This client was "bad business". He took up a lot of my time which I could have invested in marketing and prospecting for a better client.

There was also the case of a married couple that asked for quotes for life and health policies. After spending several hours working on it, they didn't return my phone calls for months. I gave up on them, only to have the wife call me a year later and tell me how desperate they were for coverage. She insisted that her husband would sign off on an application. Once again, I took the time to put together the information. The wife said that she would make her husband aware I would be coming to his workplace and that he was to sign whatever I gave him.

When he saw me walk through the door he flipped out. "What the hell do you want now?" he screamed.

"Your wife told me to come here," I replied.

"I don't know anything about this!" he barked.

I paused for a moment and took a long breath.

"You know, this is my fault. I should have called to let you know I was coming because you two have stood me up multiple times before. I should have known better than to listen to your wife again."

He sneered. "Get the hell out of here!"

"I'm leaving, but tell your wife to leave me the hell alone. I don't need business this badly."

I'll spare you the profanity laced dialog that followed but someone invited the other to some sort of amorous relationship. A few months later, I ran into the wife. She said they had gone with another agent whom they didn't like and wanted to switch to me, but only under the condition that I wouldn't "freak out again like you did to my husband." I told her I couldn't make promises and "who knows how I'll behave". I didn't take them on as clients.

Both of these cases are examples of "bad business" and why "no business" would have been better. You see, when you have no business, you can use that time to prospect for good business. I probably could have found one or two good prospects in the time I wasted with the $100 case. And the same would be true with the second example. And I could have kept my sanity as well.

So if you have no business for a day, use that time to find good business. And with some experience you will quickly spot bad business and avoid it.

DUMB STORY

Whenever a new business opens, I like to introduce myself and welcome them to the neighborhood. Generally speaking, a new business isn't going to give you much income, but I think it's a nice gesture and can plant the seed for something down the road.

So when a new mattress store opened up down the road from my office I thought nothing of sticking my head in the door. After saying hello to the owner, who was just sitting there doing nothing, I handed him my card and said, "I just came by to introduce myself. If there is anything I can do to help you succeed, please let me know." Obviously, I wasn't trying to sell the guy anything.

That's when things got ugly. This jackass started screaming about how he had just moved to the area and he wasn't making money because people were horrible for coming to his store and not buying his products. And of course, I was out of line because I was "just another salesman".

I learned a long time ago that when someone gets upset, to just sit back and watch, which is what

I did. He went off on me for a few minutes before he ran out of gas. Then I threw it back at him.

"I'm going to make a prediction," I said calmly. "I don't think you'll be in business six months from now."

"What the hell is that supposed to mean?" he screamed.

"I came here to say 'hello' and to wish you luck but you have a crappy attitude. Who's to say that I may or may not have needed some bedding in the near future, but rest assured, if I do, I won't be back here. Thanks for your time." I walked out while he called me an asshole. I let him know the sentiments were mutual. And sure enough, he and his business were gone in less than three months.

Something similar happened not long after. I was in the market for a laptop computer. I try to do business with locally owned small businesses, so I went to a neighborhood computer store. Introducing myself, I handed the nice lady at the counter my card out of habit. I told her what I was looking for and she pointed to a man in back of the store who was helping a young woman.

"He's the business owner and he can help you when he is done assisting her."

I watched as he finished talking with the customer, walked her to her car, and came back into the store. The nice sales lady handed him my card, but before she could explain to him that I was a customer, he glanced at it and decided to rip me a new one.

"What the hell is this? You want to sell me insurance? Insurance is a rip-off and I'll never buy that shit again! Not from you or anyone else."

The nice lady was waving her arms around trying to get him to shut up, but he kept telling me how my business sucked and I was probably a crook and dishonest. Again, I let him get it all out of his system until she interrupted him.

"Actually Bill, he's here to buy a computer."

Without breaking stride, the moron casually walked over to some models that were on display and began to tell me about them as if the previous conversation had never happened. Finally, he said, "Sorry about the outburst," and continued to try to sell me a computer.

I watched this train wreck keep going for as long as I could without opening my mouth. He had insulted me and my work and now it was my turn to waste his time as much as he had wasted mine.

Finally, I told him I would have to think about it. He knew he had blown the sale. Instead of contrition, I got the feeling that inside that tiny brain of his I was still the bad guy. In as calm of a voice as I could muster I said, "Sir, you don't know me and I don't know you, but given the last few minutes as evidence, I wouldn't buy a computer from you if you had the last damn computer in town." I pointed to the nice lady and said, "You should give her a raise and let her be the face of this business while you stay in the back room away from the public."

Neither of them said a word as I walked to the exit. Before the door closed all the way, I looked at the lady and said, "He's quite an asshole. I hope you are aware of that."

As I related this story to a friend a few days later, I learned that the nice lady was the guy's wife. Again, I made my fateful prediction that the business would fail within six months. I am not bragging that I am a psychic, but when people are rude to sales people, they are usually rude to customers as well. And sure enough, this business was gone in under four months.

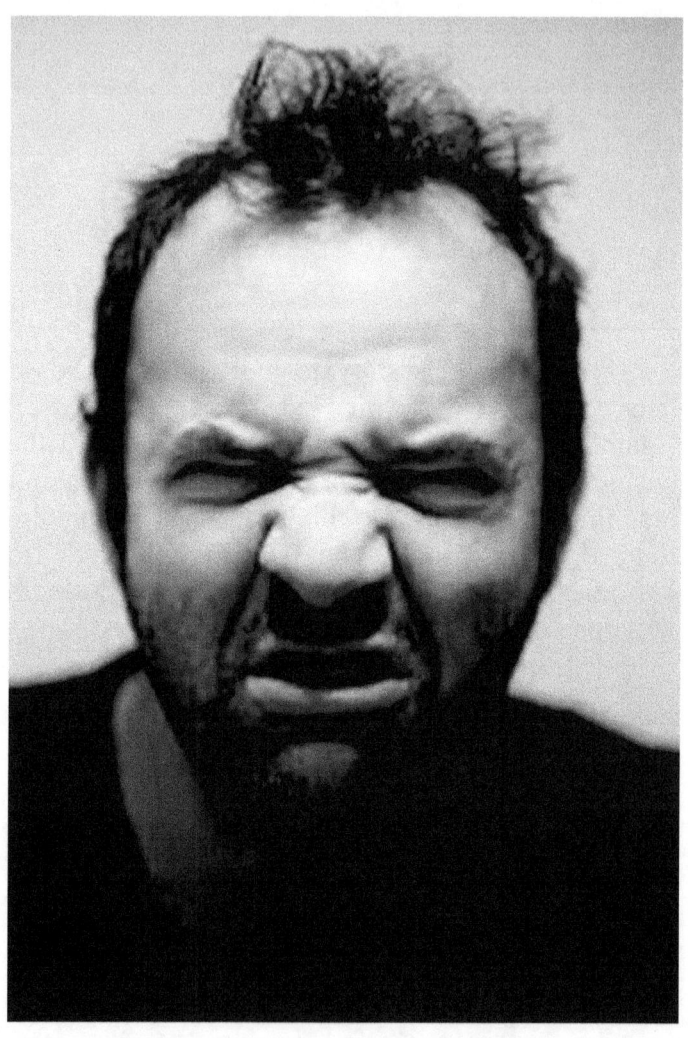

Don't be rude to sales people!

Chapter 3

WHAT IS SALES?

"Being powerful is like being a lady. If you have to tell people you are, you aren't." - **Margaret Thatcher**

Have you ever convinced someone to do something they hadn't planned on doing? If so, congratulations, you are a sales person! Especially if you got some money out of them. No matter if you upsold something or changed the customer's whole buying plan, you sold.

Imagine walking into someone's home at dinner time, unannounced no less. The wife is trying to get dinner on the table and the husband just wants to unwind and watch TV. Kids are running around because they have been in school all day and have energy they need to burn. On the surface, you would think it's a no-win situation. The last thing these people want is a salesmen in their midst. But believe me, there have been times when I walked out of that home with a check in my hand (and sometimes food in my belly)!

25

Those nice people had no intention of buying anything. I *sold* something to them. That is selling!

Envision another scenario. You work in a store and someone walks up to the register and puts a pack of gum on the counter. Smiling, you take their money, hand them a receipt and out the door they go. Did you really sell them anything? Not really.

For those of us who study the craft, there's a difference between selling and being an order taker. We need to know if the buyer is in "the buying mood". Our family at the dinner table was not in a buying mood. They wanted to get dinner on the table, relax and probably be left alone.

But the customer in the store was in a buying mood. Do you know how you can tell? Because they were in a store in the first place! A sale happened but the customer got what they originally wanted. Gum! But if you had asked, "Would you like a cup of fresh coffee to go?" and they bought that as well, then you did sell something.

I knew a property and casualty insurance agent years ago who would sell a homeowners' policy. As his customer would be walking out the door he would pump his fist and scream, "Sold!" What a jackass! And definitely *not* a salesman.

Given that the mortgage company required the policy, this agent hadn't "sold" a damn thing, he just took the order. It was merely a transaction, just like the gum purchase.

And this, my friends, is the difference between "relationship selling" and "transactional selling". Relationship selling will almost always bring you more sales because you have to build some trust, and that trust takes you from the sales zone to the trusted professional zone. When the customer wants to buy something else, which zone do you want to be in?

Did the kid at McDonald's earn your trust when you ordered that Big Mac? Doubtful. But a really good server in a decent restaurant will make a recommendation like, "I love the cheesecake. It's the best!" (This makes me want cheesecake right now.) And if you agree to the cheesecake, you've been upsold, which adds to the bill, which in turn, should make that server's tip a little better, assuming you are a good tipper.

How did the server build a relationship when the kid at McDonald's didn't? For starters, the server more than likely introduced him or herself from the beginning. A polite welcoming smile built the tiniest foundation of a relationship. That's all it took to convince you to get cheesecake.

DUMB STORY

Joe was my first real sales manager. It was obvious that he had been in the trenches as a salesman. Gruff and stern, he could be generous with his agents because he had been one as well and he knew what it was like to sell door-to-door in the middle of nowhere. He could also be a hard ass who let his anger simmer just below the surface.

He had a gin blossom from years of excessive drinking and was probably in his mid-50's. He told us he was in his 60's but I think he liked to hear how "good he looked for his age". He also liked to remind us that he had been a boxer as a teenager.

Our crew of about a dozen agents consisted mostly of recent college graduates. The new guys had tons of enthusiasm in the beginning but six months into our jobs we couldn't care less about the company. And we really didn't like our bosses, who had been less than forthcoming about the work involved.

As the end of the year drew near, we were left with nothing to do. We finished working our territory early and were concerned about not having any income for Christmas. But the excessive amount of employee turnover was about to work in our favor.

Another crew in the western part of the state had all quit around the same time and this left a territory that needed to be worked. The company paid for our accommodations at a truly disgusting motel and we were given our assignments. We didn't really try to sell additional policies, but instead just rode around picking up premiums on the existing cases. It was easy work for the most part.

But Joe was not happy. We met in a co-worker's room after work to talk and drink some beers when Joe walked in. He smelled like he had enjoyed a few cocktails as well.

"You guys are just acting like pimps! Hell, pimps are doing more selling than you idiots!" He was screaming at the top of his lungs. He was sitting on a bed in his expensive cashmere sport coat. Getting louder, he started punching the mattress and leaving a mark. Another agent, Frank, told Joe he was out of line. Joe jumped up and got nose to nose with Frank.

"Just because you're a foot taller than me doesn't mean I can't take you, sonny."

Frank looked at us and at Joe. He asked for someone to open the door and then grabbed Joe in a bear hug, holding his arms down. Frank picked up Joe, who was kicking his drunk little legs, and carried him outside, where it was damn near freezing. Holding his boss over the edge of the pool and with no emotion, he let go. Joe sank into the water.

"Oh shit!" we all said in unison. Then Joe slowly came to the surface and crawled out of the water. Steam was rising from him and he had a look on his face of anger like I have never seen since. His clothes were drenched, including that lovely sport coat. Not saying a word, he sneered at us and went to his room.

We all looked at each other and thought that Frank was a goner for sure. Hell, we may all get fired over this incident. A half hour went by as we pondered whether or not we would still have jobs. Then we heard a knock at the door.

It was Joe. He had gone to his room and taken a hot shower. Dressed in what looked like a knock off of a name brand warm up suit, he walked in.

"Sorry guys. I was out of line. I deserved what I got."

Frank looked him over. "We're cool. I'm sorry I tossed you into the pool." '

Joe told us that he sobered up as soon as he hit that cold water. But the bad news was that he had sold some policies that day, and a few people had written him checks, which were in the pocket of his sport coat. The pool water had "erased" the checks and they were now blank. Joe was going to have to go back to those customers and get new checks. And I know he wasn't going to tell them what really happened.

Drinking and selling were the two things Joe was good at. We spotted his car outside of taverns sometimes as early as 10am. I often wondered if he got hammered like he did that night at the motel and called on customers. Somehow he would always manage to sell more that the rest of us sober guys.

Chapter 4

THE STAGES OF SELLING

"Eagles soar, but weasels don't get sucked into jet engines." - **Steven Wright**

When I first began selling insurance, I was taught to drop in, most likely unannounced, do a presentation, and close the sale. If the prospect put up an objection, I was supposed to dig into a vast catalog of rebuttals. And by "vast" I mean a 3-ring binder stuffed with comebacks that we were supposed to memorize and use with enthusiasm.

"I don't have any money to buy your accident plan with," I would hear.

"Well, ma'am, if you don't have money now then what will you do if you had an accident and couldn't work?" I would say forcefully. "You'll really be in trouble!"

Needless to say, we were supposed to get the sale on the first visit. In retrospect, this was a crazy way of selling. Where was the rapport? Where was the trust? Where was the relationship selling? The relationship didn't exist. I was selling a crappy policy that cost $30 for six months. It was purely a transactional sale.

There isn't a high level of "stickiness" or persistency in transactional sales. In other words, that business doesn't stay on the books long because the client will stop making payments. This is vitally important when you are selling a product that yields a "residual" income. On the other hand, if you are a realtor, once the buyer makes the purchase you don't give a rat's ass after they make their first mortgage payment.

The first stage of selling is **prospecting**. We need to find people to talk to. And we try to "qualify" our prospects by getting some information. Does this person have a job? Do they have kids? What is the age of this person? Is this a person we want to deal with? How about a criminal record?

Prospecting can happen in various ways. You can send out mailers, ask for referrals, show up at networking events or even knock on doors at a trailer park. Just go where the people are! Take any opportunity to find someone that can benefit from your product or service.

Just getting a name isn't enough, so you will want to meet your prospect in person. Personally, I prefer making an appointment. It's an easy way to let people know that I am a professional and will treat them as such. Offer to meet your prospect at a local coffee shop. Some people can be anxious about meeting a stranger, so a public spot is good. There are too many weirdos out there. And *always* treat! This isn't the time to look like a cheapskate.

During the appointment, your goal is to ask some open ended questions to get a conversation started. Some rookies will actually pull out a questionnaire and read questions off of it. I prefer to have my questions ready in my head. As the prospect begins answering my questions, I'll ask "Is it okay with you if I make some notes?" These notes will provide me with enough information to surmise if this person has a need for me or my services. And specifically what kind of parameters I need to work within, like "Are you broke? If you are, I'm probably wasting my time right now."

Realtors can ask questions pertaining to income, family size and *budget*. If you are selling advertising, you can ask about their target market and the client's *budget*. Auto dealers will always ask their customers about taste in cars and, of course, the *budget*. Are you seeing a pattern yet?

No matter what type of selling you do, the customer will always have a budget in mind. This is what your customer wants to spend and your job is to figure out how to work within it. And if it's unrealistic, the best bet is to tell your client upfront.

"I don't want to keep you from doing business with us but you're going to have a difficult time finding a full-size SUV with all of the extras for $5000."

Believe it or not, there are a lot of people who just don't know what things cost. They are either mentally stuck in the prices of their youths or think the price of everything is through the roof. You will have to get them back on track.

The goal of all of this is to **open your sale**. Let the prospect know that you have discovered a need and will do your best to find a solution that will fit in their budget. Recapping and confirming the important parts of the conversation helps your prospect understand what is going to happen next.

"Mr. Carter, you said that you have a dozen employees and would like to offer them some benefits so they'll stick around. Also, you don't want to spend more than $100 per month on each person. Is that correct?"

"Yes it is."

At this point I may have a solution ready and will try to **close the sale.** I may say to the prospect, "We can take care of this quickly and easily. When would you like to get it started?" The part where I ask when to start was the "assumptive close", as I am assuming that Mr. Carter is going to buy. I could have asked another question like, "How would you like to make your payments?"

Don't be afraid to go down this road. It's brazen yet subtle. Kids do it all the time. "Dad, were you taking me to the movie or the mall today?" I didn't know I had offered either, but somehow I just got a binary choice.

For me, it typically takes a few appointments and a couple of attempts to close the sale before getting the sale. This is because I truly want to take the time to find out what is needed. Sometimes they don't even know what they need, but having a conversation with your prospect can work miracles.

Many years ago I had a client who was a cosmetologist. I asked her what her professional goals were and she said that she wanted to open a beauty school (what they were called back in the day). When I asked her for specifics, she looked confused.

"How much would it cost to open this school?" I asked.

"I don't know," she replied. "I never thought of that part'"

So we broke it down the best we could. We estimated the costs of chairs, towels, sinks, mirrors, brooms, supplies, insurance and taxes. I'm not sure we were even in the correct ballpark on many of the numbers she came up with, but it was more information than she had before our conversation.

"You know, I never went through that process before. At least now I have a rough idea of how much money I will need to get this off the ground," she said with a serious look. And if the numbers were not accurate, at least she has begun the process of thinking her way to her goal.

Back to closing, the sales curve can be short or long depending on what you are selling. Realtors may need to show several homes before getting an offer or a contract. It's rare for me to close the sale on a first visit, unless someone knows exactly what they want to buy. For others, opening and closing can happen in one meeting.

You can make multiple attempts at closing. Just like when you were dating, you didn't give up on the first, second or third try. "Hang in there for three!" is the slogan we have for the amount of rejection one should take at the hands of a prospect.

DUMB STORY

Working as a contract enroller is fairly easy in that the employees of a work place will sign up for individual meeting times. The meeting takes a few minutes to review their benefits and make any necessary changes.

The downside to the job is the travel. After spending a week several hundred miles from home, I look forward to leaving a location on Friday afternoon for the long drive home.

As is my luck, one Friday a man walked in around lunch time and asked me what times were available to meet. I tried suggesting earlier times but this numb nuts signed up for the last time slot at 4pm. Seriously?

When his time came around, I waited and waited. I stood outside of the small conference room looking for this moron. "I'm not going to get home until midnight," I muttered under my breath.

A nice lady I had spoken to earlier came down the hallway and asked me if I needed help. I told her who I was looking for and she said, "He left around 2:00. Was he supposed to meet with you?"

She had a look that said she knew what a prick this guy was. I thanked her and packed my computer and got the hell out of there. I eventually made it home at 11:58.

Chapter 5

YOUR MENTAL STATE

"Be backs aren't greenbacks." - John DeHaven, sales manager, TruGreen

As we have already discussed, selling can be a lonely and depressing job. Constantly getting rejected by prospects while managers expect more sales can wear you down mentally. Add to that any other baggage such as fear of public speaking, family issues or financial concerns and the job can take a huge toll on you emotionally and physically. You may notice that your co-workers are dropping like flies and that turnover is constant.

If your employers have any common sense, they'll see it too. Most sales managers have been in your shoes. The good ones will do their best to keep you motivated, positive and continue to encourage you. You will need to take the initiative and do some of this on your own.

Enthusiasm is contagious. If you are enthused about your work, others will be as well. Good realtors *love* to talk about great neighborhoods, home values and mortgage rates. If they see a property that can be a good investment, they will share that information excitedly with you.

Being enthused doesn't mean you have to jump up and down with vim and vigor. People don't have to see your passion for your work because they will sense it. It's more like a simmering feeling you will exude. With that said, even the most low-key, introverted people can be enthused about their work.

I know sales reps that are as quiet as a church mouse in public and are the last ones you would suspect of being successful. But when you get these folks in a one-on-one situation they will suddenly become talkative and a show a level of emotion you never knew was there. Just because they aren't over the top and pushy doesn't mean they aren't passionate about their work.

Attitude is key. Thinking positive and being confident are vital. Don't confuse this with being cocky. No one likes an arrogant jerk. For many people starting in sales, having to show confidence without being cocky is new territory. This explains why the public perceives sellers as pushy and high pressure. Newbies sometimes try too hard.

There are many programs out there to help boost your confidence and some will work for you, but *the foundation of confidence is having some small successes to build from.* People who are genuinely confident will exude a positive attitude also, and both are a result from knowing that goals, no matter how small, can be attained. Once I hit a sales goal, I no longer doubt if it can be attained. But if I set a goal too high, I will continue to feel that the goal is out of reach. Set reasonable goals, get success, build your confidence and then raise the goal again.

The result of all of this is improving your overall attitude. I once had a manager who would put his index fingers on either side of his head, point to his temples and say "all of your problems are between these six inches in your skull." As much as I disliked the guy, he was right sometimes and this was one of those times.

Stay motivated and do it often. Okay, this sentence makes no sense, so let me explain. Many of us who get into sales need motivation to keep going. There are plenty of motivational speakers out there. Most sales organizations worth their salt will have meetings and seminars featuring such speakers. If your company doesn't, utilize YouTube. There are plenty of videos available from TED talks to sports coaches. Schedule a time to enjoy them.

The problem I see with all of this is that you'll hear someone speak, get gung-ho about work, and then fizzle out after a week or so. I like to refer to it as a temporary "motivation high". That's why I say to "do it often".

As a side note, if you think you would like to be on the other side of this and actually be a motivational speaker that is great too! But what if you aren't a great speaker? No problem. I highly recommend you investigate your local Toastmasters group. In exchange for very reasonable dues, you will be given the tools to work on your speaking skills at your own pace and in a "safe" environment. Remember that the other members of the club were once where you are. Everyone encourages each other and the meetings are fun and informative.

Find a work/life balance. Selling can feel like a 24 hour job. You can't clock out because you never know when or where your next client or customer will find you. But to avoid getting burned out, you'll have to find some time to decompress. Much like a lightbulb you can't always be "on", but rather find a way to hit the dimmer switch.

I met a successful insurance agent who told me that once a year he would go on a private vacation without anyone else. He would leave his wife and kids at home and go to a cabin or a beach. He used that time to get rid of stress (yes, family causes stress), read, meditate and recharge his batteries..

In case you think he was awful for leaving his family behind, let me calm your worries. His wife fully understood the importance of this for him. And he was successful enough to afford a lovely vacation with his entire family in addition to his own sabbatical.

Find support. A successful salesperson is only as good as their support team. Much like a quarterback depends on his offensive line, you will need several people to guide you, train you and offer advice. Very often, this team will consist of a group of people who don't interact, or in my case, even know each other. I have one fellow who helps me with Medicare products, another who helps me with prospecting and marketing, and an assortment of others who are there if I need help in areas I'm not familiar with. I don't keep in contact with them until I need them, but they are at arm's length just in case.

I also recommend that you find a mentor. Some companies will assign one to you, but if you don't have one, get one. I was fortunate enough to have a veteran of the business take me under his wing and give solid advice whenever I needed it. He also had an unusual habit of randomly calling me at 6am to make sure I was ready to work. I wasn't, but it didn't stop him from giving me the occasional wake up call.

Your support team should be there for you when you need training. With the advent of the internet, most of this can now be done remotely through webinars. However, if your manager sends you a brochure and a CD-ROM and refers to it as a "sales training kit", you may want to find other options.

Remember that training you costs money and someone is expecting a return on that investment. I've worked for companies that put me in a conference room for three days reading manuals, and I have also worked with others that had a year-long program with homework and follow up sessions. Obviously it varies from company to company.

Take time to notice is how often training is offered and how many people are going through the process. My first insurance job held a two week training class, followed by a week of studying for our state license exam. There were about forty people in that class and through casual conversation with the instructor I found out that this was done twelve times a year. It didn't take much math skills to realize that this company had a lot of turnover! If the job was as great as they billed it to be, the sales force wouldn't have been hemorrhaging.

Generally speaking, the best support team is there for you when you need them, even if it means having someone to answer a quick question via telephone or email.

Compartmentalize your business. Break your work into segments to see which ones work for you and which ones don't. When I managed a retail store, we would try to maximize our sales per square foot. If we had committed 20 feet of wall space to a product line, and it was getting half the sales of another product line with 10 feet of wall space, we could make the adjustment.

You can do this with your own business as well. For instance, I have offered several lines of insurance and I allot a certain amount of time to each one. I don't want to spend 30% of my time working on Long Term Care cases that only bring me 5% of my income. But if my group benefits sales comprise 70% of my income and only taking up 10% of my time, I should probably try to double the time investment on that.

By compartmentalizing your products, you can tell which ones are dogs and which ones are flying out the door. Do the math and be objective. Believe it or not there are salespeople out there who form an emotional attachment to a product and will rationalize that a sales dog is a "loss leader" and must stay in the line-up. This is akin to keeping your aging quarterback in the game because he's a fan favorite, despite the fact he can't throw the ball and his knees are shot.

Don't play checkers, play chess. We can't afford to just think about the next move. In today's business environment we need to think several moves ahead. Consider what your competition is doing, as well as the moves of your client. Short sighted sales people play checkers. Successful sales professionals play chess.

*How are you planning to succeed?   Are you
playing chess or checkers?*

DUMB STORY

Have you ever seen the bumper sticker that reads, "I owe, I owe, so off to work I go"? In my case, I owed because of work.

After being out of the insurance industry for a few years I went to work for a worksite benefits company. They were eager to pay our commissions in advance and never mentioned in the training there were other options, including "as earned" which meant that I would get paid when the company got paid.

The owner of a small motel agreed to let me offer some benefits to his housekeeping staff on a payroll deduction basis. Finally I was going to make a few dollars!

After a brief presentation on the products, a few women came to the motel's breakfast area one at a time and each purchased a cancer plan or a disability policy. They were pleasant and grateful that I took the time to explain everything in detail.

A week later I walked out to my mailbox to find a check for $450. I quickly deposited it with the intention of paying some bills. With all of that money burning a hole in my pocket I even treated myself to a Happy Meal.

About two weeks after enrolling the housekeeping staff I rode by the motel again to thank the owner for his help. Solemnly, he broke the news to me.

"They quit. They all quit." He didn't look too concerned about this turn of events. "They got mad at me for something they thought I said or did. Who knows and who cares? They were all related. Cousins and sisters and when one got mad at me they all got mad and walked out." He also let me know that this all went down a few days after my last visit, which meant he never deducted any of the premiums from their paychecks.

Confusion set in. I had already been paid and spent the money. And now I was going to get hit with a chargeback for the full amount. This really sucked!

I learned later that I could have applied for a code that would have given me an "as earned" commission but apparently our management team didn't tell us about it because they were paid in the same manner as we were. A veteran agent told me, "Everyone knows that when it comes to housekeepers, waiters and dishwashers, you go 'as earned'. Those people quit their jobs after three or four months. You're going to get killed with chargebacks."

And that is how I began the second phase of my insurance career in the hole for $450. Most people would have taken it as a sign, but I'm apparently a glutton for punishment.

Chapter 6

THE WORLD'S BEST PICKUP LINE

"Sometimes I feel like a square peg living in a world of round holes." - Lori White, award winning realtor

We have already established that there are people in this business who are more successful than others. And the ones that succeed have overcome their fear of being told "no". There is actually a school of thought that says that for every "no" you get, the closer you are to a "yes". The logic is that if you don't give up and can handle rejection, you'll succeed.

The problem with this is that hearing "no" all the time can wear you down. Your confidence will drop and the next thing you know you're killing time doing things that just aren't productive. After a few days you realize you have nothing to show for your hours on Facebook or Twitter, making you even more depressed.

Having no prospects in your pipeline, you have to hit the streets or work the phone to start cold calling. Cold calling is approaching a person or a business "cold", with no introduction or even a name to get you in the door. Some people love to cold call. I am not one of them.

"I'm not interested," is the refrain you'll hear over and over again. Most people will try to be polite. Others consider it a badge of honor to tell their friends "I threw a salesman out of my office today!" Either way, the amount of rejection can suck the life out of you quickly.

To get around this, we have to acknowledge that this business is mental. All of your potential for success is between your temples, that six inches between your ears. Any limitations we have are imagined.

People will be rude. And they will find stupid reasons not to buy from you. They may not like your appearance or the tone of your voice. Apparently facial hair can be a factor as well as baldness. I once had an idiot ask me what kind of car I drove. (He approved of my Chrysler) Some people will only buy from "locals". Others don't want anyone from their town to know their business and only feel comfortable buying from the person one town over. There is no rhyme or reason for any of it.

Let's get back to our reluctance to talk to people and how to overcome the fear. Being turned away is like a punch to the gut, but instead it hurts in another part of our bodies – our pride. We establish alibis for not wanting to continue because it's painful. Most of us aren't masochists.

We have to learn to market ourselves better. How can we be assertive without being aggressive? How can you look knowledgeable without coming off as arrogant? How can you attract business by being a magnet instead of that person everyone wants to avoid?

When I was single, my friends and I would develop horrible pick-up lines to use at clubs and bars, and since the females weren't amused by us, we would mostly try to amuse ourselves. The worst included:

"Didn't I see you in Rome last week driving a Porsche like mine?"
"My mansion is right around the corner."
"Does this smell like chloroform?" (Okay, that one is just creepy.)

Eventually we found a line that actually worked. *"I thrive on rejection. Will you go out with me?"* Do you see what I did there? I made a win/win situation out of it. Sneaky, huh?

If the young lady agrees to go on a date, the line worked. But if she turns me down, my pride isn't hurt. As a matter of fact, I'll even enjoy it a little. Sure, it's a little twisted, but takes away the sting of rejection.

If you use this concept in sales (what is a harder sell than convincing someone to accompany you on a date?) you can keep low morale at bay. Do you remember what I said earlier about how hard this job is?   Any trick that you can use to keep your head in the game is good.   And humor is a great way to not let yourself get down.

I once heard an interview with George Foreman on the radio.   He said he was "always selling" and you know he was selling with that giant smile on his face.

Are you keeping a smile on your face when you meet people?   Are you willing to "thrive on rejection"?   This doesn't mean you are asking to be turned down.   Give it your best shot, but don't take a little rejection to heart.   And a little masochism and self-deprecating humor can make it sting a little less.

DUMB STORY

I was sent to collect some insurance premiums from an elderly couple living in rural North Carolina.   The house was about a quarter of a mile off the highway and the driveway was really a short dirt road.   As I was pulling in, a car passed me going pretty fast and kicking up dirt.   "Damn," I thought to myself, "these people are leaving.   I don't want to have to come back later."

Maybe someone would be home.   I rang the bell and a very pissed off lady came to the door.

"What do you want?"   She said tersely.   "You're with that other guy, aren't you?"

"No ma'am," I said, recalling the car leaving.   "I

don't know who that guy was." She was looking me up and down and I knew I had to calm her down. "You already have this policy. I just came by to pick up your premium."

She pointed to the den where I saw her husband in a recliner with a pistol on the end table next to him. He looked at me, waved the gun around and said, "Oh shit, another one?" He also assumed that I worked with the guy that flew by me in the driveway.

After a few minutes of doing my best to calm them down and not shoot me, I got a better explanation of what had transpired a few minutes before I arrived. The other guy was selling vacuum cleaners and wouldn't take "no" for an answer. After many objections, the idiot threw dirt on their carpet to demonstrate his product, and this was the final straw for the old man, who pulled his pistol out to chase the salesman off.

As the couple told me what had happened, I could tell they were quite embarrassed as to how I had been treated. They ended up being extremely nice people. They even bought a couple more policies from me and fed me lunch. Then the old man took out to see his bull in barn. These were great people who had been treated badly.

I have always thought of that incident as a success story. I took a horrible situation and made it awesome. And when a vacuum cleaner salesman comes to my house I share the story with them.

Not my client

Chapter 7

YOU ARE YOUR BRAND

"If you don't have an appointment you are unemployed." - Willie Kee, Benefits Specialist

As I mentioned earlier, people buy from you because they like and trust you. If you are a realtor, they think of you as the expert in real estate and will forever be grateful for your knowledge on related subjects, such as mortgages or home inspections. You have a certain sphere of influence in your industry. And the same goes for attorneys, doctors and used car salespeople.

Let's say your next door neighbor is a well-regarded tax accountant who specializes in corporate accounts. You would love to bend his ear periodically on general tax issues as well as his specific work. But what would your response be if he told you that he was joined a multi-level marketing (MLM) group and was selling travel vouchers and thinks you should too?

What do travel vouchers have to do with his work? Is he desperate for money? And why is he trying to sign me up to sell travel vouchers too? These are the questions that you should be asking yourself.

It doesn't matter if you work for a big company with a name behind you, or if you are self-employed. *Your name is your brand!* When people hear your name, they associate you with your work. So when you get into a business that has nothing to do with what you're known for, you water down your name brand.

On the other hand, if you have a hobby or charity that you are known for supporting, that's great. But make sure the public is aware that your enthusiasm for helping homeless pets isn't taking away from your work.

Johnson & Johnson have been in the business of marketing their lines of personal care products for many years. That's what they are known for. Would you take them seriously if they rolled out a line of greeting cards? Probably not.

When people think of you, what do they think of? Do they think of you as an expert in your industry or do they think of the person that is spread out selling something completely different every time they see you?

For some reason, people incorrectly assume that because I'm in sales, I would want to sell their wares as well. I sell insurance, not cell phones or security systems or anything else that's not related to insurance or financial products.

After the financial crisis of 2008, I noticed a lot

of people who had lost their jobs and were now representing various multi-level marketing (MLM's) organizations. They paid a franchise fee for the right to sell someone's product. And anyone else could do the same also, so they didn't have any exclusive rights or a territory. Other than the occasional sales rally and motivational talks, they weren't getting much value for their money.

I know plenty of people who love this business model and have had success. However, my main concern when talking to these people is they are being told they are becoming "business owners", when in reality it's a sales job they are taking on.

A good franchise would make sure you could succeed, not just take your fees. It's been said that McDonald's isn't a food business, but a real estate business because they want to insure that their franchisees are in locations to maximize their sales. They also have great name recognition. In essence that is what you are paying for.

But remember that you're branding yourself as well. Do you want to be known as the person that "also sells diet plans on the side"? Is this venture really going to give you an extra additional stream or is it just going to make your friends and family avoid you like the plague? More questions you should ask yourself.

We have all heard the expression, "You have to spend money to make money." It can be true. I personally reinvest a portion of my income back into my business for marketing, gasoline for my vehicle, taking clients out for coffee, etc. And there are plenty of legitimate franchises out that require you to make an upfront investment as a business owner.

A few years ago, I met a married couple who had tried to make it in the music business. They were really talented but having a difficult time getting noticed in a small town. We chatted and exchanged phone numbers. About a year later I got a phone call one evening from the husband.

He had signed up as a rep for an MLM and wanted to enlist me. I could hear the desperation in his voice over the phone as he told me how awesome this would be for me. Was he trying to convince me or himself? I wasn't interested but I tried to be nice to the guy, so I asked him how much he was making.

"Enough to make my mortgage payment," he said defiantly.

"Really?" I asked. "I'll make you a deal then. Call me back in six months. If you can show me check stubs verifying that number, I'll sign up."

Six months went by and I heard nothing. A year or so later, I ran into him and his wife at a bookstore. They looked down in the dumps. It was obvious that the venture into the MLM was a sore subject and I didn't want to be an ass and rub his nose in it.

"How's it going?" I asked. "You guys doing okay?"

He nodded passively. "Yeah, we've decided to make some changes. Maybe even get back into music." I sincerely wished him luck.

These were nice people who got suckered. And as I said earlier, someone presented the MLM to them as a great business deal, instead of a sales job. And the harsh reality was that these people were not salespeople. They did not have an ounce of selling DNA in their bones, as was obvious in our phone conversation.

Some people are outgoing and extroverted and when they die, you hear how they never met a stranger. Those people are great at selling. Others just aren't good at it and contrary to what sales/recruiting managers say, no matter how much training and encouragement you give them, they never will succeed at sales. "You're going to be great at this!" just doesn't work.

DUMB STORY

In college, I played bass guitar (poorly) and some friends wanted to start a band. We had a guitar player who was older than us and had been in several groups years earlier. Acknowledging our limitations, we gave up on playing in nightclubs and decided to look for exposure elsewhere. (This means were so bad we couldn't get hired to play for free.)

Someone mentioned a Battle of the Bands competition at a local venue. The required entry fee of $100 seemed a bit steep. Our veteran guitar player sighed and said, "You guys can throw away your money but I'll never pay someone to play my guitar. I get paid to play, not the other way around."

I always remembered that comment and considered it when someone would approach me to sell for them. Ask yourself, "Why am I paying for the privilege to sell this product and shouldn't it be the other way around? Shouldn't they be paying me?"

Note: Our band never had any groupies but we did go through a series of name changes. This usually happened after playing publicly so as to spare our friends and families from the shame and humiliation of knowing us.

I did learn a little bit about marketing during this time. I composed a completely fake history of our band, including phony biographies about each member. I had them printed and distributed them to each member of the band.

Our guitarist, who worked for a radio station, left a stack of the fliers sitting on his desk where a record label representative happened to see them. "I've never heard of these guys before. Are they local?"

The guitarist laughed and had to explain it wasn't a real band, just us making a feeble attempt to get a gig. The label rep appreciated the effort, but when he heard us play he said he'd make sure no one would have to suffer through listening to us. At least we thrived on rejection.

Chapter 8

GETTING YOUR MESSAGE TO THE MASSES

"Beware the lollipop of mediocrity; lick it once and you'll suck forever. - Brian Wilson

This is most likely going to be the longest chapter in this book for one simple reason: If you are in sales, you will be spending a vast majority of your time looking for someone to talk to.

You are going to need to find a way to let people know what you are offering. Luckily, you can do this on the cheap if you have a little guidance and some perseverance. As an amateur guru in the practices of marketing, I'd like to share some pointers and some of my own experiences.

First and foremost, *not all forms of marketing work for all industries*. Regardless of what the nice lady selling Yellow Pages ads says, there's a good chance you'll be throwing your money away. I recommend you take a look at what other successful people in your industry are doing to market themselves and copy it. This may seem like common sense, but if other car dealerships are on TV and radio, that's probably where you should be.

Why not try something different, like a billboard? Because it's probably been done before and just didn't work. But a billboard may work for another industry. My point is that you are not going to be the first to try the Yellow Pages in your industry, but you may be stuck with an expensive ad that may not get you customers.

For instance, in my industry, insurance and financial products, you don't see a lot of TV or radio advertising. "Come on down to Big Bob's House of Life Insurance!" That would just look silly. While you may see commercials for companies, you don't see a lot for individual agents. What does work for me? Word of mouth. Again, I am my brand.

Successful people in my industry do a lot of networking and working from referrals. This may not be the case if you sell linens to restaurants or are a wholesaler for an extreme sports brand.

Speaking of the Yellow Pages, have you looked in there lately? You should notice which industries buy up large parts of the pages. Attorneys and exterminators apparently do great, but banks and upholstery cleaners, not so much.

So, if you're considering a large ad on the side of a bus, find out if anyone in your industry is doing this too.

Budget

The cost of advertising is tricky. That whole "you have to spend money to make money" thing rears its head again. What percentage of your profits do you want to reinvest in marketing? If you are just starting out you won't have a clue because you won't have any sales to speak of, so consider it a "startup cost".

More importantly is the "return on investment" or ROI. You should be getting back what you put in *plus more*. You should decide on a minimum ROI on your advertising to make sure it is working for you. For example, if you have a hair salon and you spend $300 on advertising, you should be getting at least 4 times that amount in business. That $300 should get you a *minimum* of $1200. If you get less, then stop and find another way to get your message out. (Opinions vary. Some people say the ROI minimum is 7 times the investment)

You can keep track of how your advertising is doing for you. Try a coupon that has a code on it. For example, if you buy a ad in the Yellow Pages with a coupon, have a "YP" coded in the corner of the ad so you'll know where it came from when it is redeemed.

Let's get back to our hair example. If you were to only get $300 worth of business, you've just worked for free. You spent $300 and got it back, plus you spent your time and energy to do someone's hair. This is why it is so important to track your marketing as much as possible. If not a coupon, try a "New Client Intake Form" or just ask,

"How did you hear about me?" Every bit of information you get is going to help in the long run.

Prospecting and Networking

Before I jump into this part I want to make one point very clear. Your goal when prospecting and networking is to meet people. The more you meet, the more you will sell. By meeting people, you will form relationships which lead to referrals, which I'll discuss later.

In the beginning of your sales career, you are going to be doing a lot of prospecting and networking. This means cold calling (which is horrible and does make you "thrive on rejection"). Again, consider the costs to you for these things. You may not want to drive around in a rural area when gas prices are high unless you are confident that you'll make that gas money back and then some.

When I cold call, I try to make it as efficient as possible by targeting strip centers. By doing this, I can park my car and walk around. Also, I can talk to people where they work, which means they have jobs. People with jobs are much better at paying their premiums each month.

I used to work with another agent who loved to hit trailer parks. He would get all kinds of sales, but the client would quickly cancel the policy or let it lapse. If you are selling to someone who is home all day watching reruns of "Sanford and Son", odds are good they aren't paying the bills. You're going to want the person in who is either working or paying the bills.

A gentleman I know sells radio advertising. We call him a "professional visitor" because he loves to drop in on businesses unannounced to "shoot the breeze". While the business owner is trying to service his clients, the radio guy will give him all of the latest gossip, get in his way and generally be a pain in the ass. The business owner won't buy advertising from him despite attempts to "wear him down".

If you do want to drop in on a prospect, make it brief and don't get in the way. A better idea is to phone ahead and try to book an appointment. If your prospect won't commit to a time, ask if you can drop in when it's "a slow time".

Networking groups are a great way to meet people. There are some amazing networking groups you can join that will cost you nothing. I have found a couple in my area on meetup.com. These groups may have some sort of a format, may or may not require dues, and can have an eclectic mix of members. Ask if you can visit a few times as a "guest" before you commit your dollars and time.

Remember that dues to groups should be treated the same as other marketing expenses. You should be getting 4 times what you are putting in at a *bare minimum*. And if there are no dues, *consider your time and put a value on it*. The time you are spending in these meetings can be more productive elsewhere if all you are doing is being social.

Before I go much deeper into the groups, I would be remiss if I didn't mention your local chamber of commerce. The chamber can offer you an extremely easy way to meet people who are business owners, professionals and other influencers. (A great way to avoid the "Sanford and Son" clientele.) Many have events on a weekly basis if you know where and how to find them, which will give you many opportunities meet these people.

I joined my chamber's "ambassador" program to maximize my interaction with other members. As an ambassador, we were assigned a portion of the membership list, usually 75-100 members. We were expected to send them an email monthly letting them know what events were scheduled, such as ribbon cuttings and Business After Hours. Also, these members were told to expect us to come by their businesses once a year with a survey, which asked basic questions, like "Do you think the chamber is working for you?" and "Do you have any suggestions to improve the chamber?"

This gave me an excellent excuse to "drop in" on a business owner that I had never met before and introduce myself. I would quickly get the survey out of the way and move on to asking about their business. This kind of conversation starter would sometimes change that member into a client.

Another advantage I had as an ambassador was getting my foot in the door early when new businesses would open. Many new business owners join the chamber for the same reasons you should – to network and meet other people who also have the same kinds of experiences. We had a monthly new member orientation for these people where they could learn all about the chamber. Again, I would attend each month, mainly to get to these people first.

But the real kick in the pants was attending the ribbon cuttings. These events varied greatly, but most would happen around lunch time, with some finger foods or light snacks, a giant pair of scissors and a large ribbon, of course. Here again, showing support for these people was a great way to make a super impression. For the most part, I thoroughly enjoyed attending ribbon cuttings and many times it resulted in a new client for me.

Ironically, there were times when we would have a ribbon cutting for a new restaurant and they wouldn't even offer a glass of water, but on the flipside, an engineering firm or a law practice would treat us to a full spread of food.

Activity is the key. If your pipeline is full, and you have plenty of appointments set, you are staying active. Does your calendar have a lot of empty spaces? If so, then you may want to work those phones. "Smilin' and dialin'" can get your book filled quickly.

Remember that sales is purely a numbers game. If you have enough prospects, you will set more appointments. And a certain percentage of those appointments will become customers. When I first started out, we were told to give a minimum of ten presentations a day. If you don't have someone to talk to, find someone.

You must keep your pipeline full. Making sure

you have enough prospects is key to your success. A veteran agent used to say "You should be seeing people or fighting to see people." My old friend, Johnny Fryar, will tell you that 'the hardest part of the job is finding someone to talk to".

A mistake many sales professionals make is having a successful sale and celebrating by taking their foot off the gas for a few days off. Why would someone do this when there is obvious momentum? There is plenty of time to slow down on Friday afternoon when no one wants to see you. Until then, I suggest you keep moving forward, working to keep your pipeline full.

Whale Hunting Whale hunting is when you spend the bulk of your time looking for large clients or accounts. Just think, if you can land one big whale, you can live off of the results for a while. Or you can continue to look for those easy-to-find smaller clients and keep the status quo.

So why wouldn't you go find your whale? For some people, it's a matter of intimidation. Let's go back to our dating analogy. A guy might think that the most attractive girl in town won't have anything to do with him. "She's too pretty for me!" he'll complain. Probably, but he'll never know if he doesn't ask. Consider this to be Schrödinger's girlfriend.

But the problem isn't that she's "too pretty" for him, but that he's afraid he'll get turned down. In his brain, he envisions a scenario where his friends mercilessly mock him for thinking he could attain the unattainable. Of course it's all between his ears.

And if she had said "yes", his stock would rise and he would begin his search for better friends.

Working your normal clientele doesn't keep you from looking for the occasional whale. When you spot your whale, keep a few things in mind:

You aren't the only one after the whale. Trust me when I say that everyone wants that doctor, lawyer or Indian chief's business. You'll need to find a way to get access to your prospect without stalking at the country club.

The sales curve can be a bit longer. Relationship selling is going to take precedence over transactional selling with these people and for most of us, it will take a considerable amount of time to penetrate this market.

Once you start the actual process of working with your whale, you'll notice that you spend just as much time working on their case as you would on much smaller one. Hell, it may even be less time, because most whales are far more organized that small fish and will help you expedite things to get your sale through faster. (They didn't get to be whales by being sloppy and inefficient.)

Whales know other whales. The law of attraction states that "like attracts like". You can put this law to your advantage if you play your cards correctly, because a couple of referrals in the high-end market can be a great meal ticket!

DUMB STORY

Each month our chamber held a Business After Hours event, which would start around 5pm and last for a few hours. Most of the attendees were coming straight from work and just wanted to eat some food, drink an adult beverage or two, and mingle with their cohorts. Of course, it didn't always work that way.

There was one couple that would eat and start drinking heavily. After an hour or so, these two would be hammered and somehow became people repellent. I admit that I was guilty of seeing them and walking in an opposite direction several times. I also love a good train wreck sometimes.

One time another ambassador brought her friend as a guest. This lovely lass definitely wasn't a business professional in any sense of the world, but it didn't stop her from drinking her weight in beer and telling all of us about her sexual prowess. After that evening we never saw her again, but there were a few of us who continued to discuss what a great member she would have made.

When you try to calculate the ROI of your chamber membership, only consider the business you get and not the amount of food and drink you consume.

Types of Networking Groups

There are "exclusive" and "non-exclusive" groups out there and it really depends on your preferences. The "exclusive" groups are structured to have one member only from an industry. For example, there will be only one realtor, one attorney, one baker, etc. The strict rule in this scenario is that the members of the group send referrals to each other instead of non-members.

But what if that exclusive travel agent (the only one in the group to refer) sucks at their job? What if they never return phone calls or are rude or don't know what they are talking about? The person who refers them gets bitten in the ass every time.

"You gave me Bob Smith's number and he's an idiot!" is what you'll hear a week later.

This has happened to me on more than one occasion after I gave referral which ended up badly. I had to do some following up.

"Did you call Mrs. Johnson back on that referral I gave you 2 weeks ago?"

"I've been meaning to but I've been busy." Not what I want to hear, and rest assured I won't be sending any more leads his way.

On the other hand, there could be a legitimate reason. Sometimes the client drops the ball.

"I've left her three messages and gave up because I don't want to pester the lady." This happens more often than you would think.

A few years back I joined an "exclusive" group. In my opinion it wasn't structured very well. We would go around the room and everyone would give "referrals", which were actually just names of businesses that had changed ownership or management. I brought in some actual warm referrals, which meant that the customer was awaiting a phone call. In the six months I was in this group, I never once received a lead and saw no ROI. It was a waste of my time but a lesson learned.

I have some friends and professional contacts

that absolutely love being in an exclusive group. They reap great rewards from the referrals. Several realtors and attorneys I know have mostly good things to say, but will admit that the atmosphere can be "political" from time to time.

And be aware that in many cases, these groups can require a commitment of your time, as they meet on a weekly basis and have expectations of you to bring in names of prospects.

"Non-exclusive" groups can be very good too. My favorite networking group has no dues, no directors, no fines if you don't show up or show up empty handed (without a referral) and meets once a month. I've been asked to speak to this group and have gotten some great leads from it.

The downside to non-exclusive groups is that there will several people in the group who are competitors, including yours. A web designer complained that he didn't like having to pitch his business while other web designers were doing the same. My thoughts were that this guy needed to grow up. We have to compete in the real world so do it in the group as well.

Having your competitors in the room makes you work a little harder mentally, especially when you have to explain to the group members why you think your business is better. It can be awkward when your competitor is sitting at the next table.

In "free" groups, you will meet people that won't do business with you. Many are self-employed and work independently from their homes. But these folks may know others who need your products or services.

If you are new to the group, take it all in stride and hang in there. No one wants to do business with someone who shows up once never to be seen again. And realize that your main purpose isn't to do business with the other members of the group per se, but instead to make yourself referable.

The Absolute Best Way to Work a Networking Room

So what do you do when you get to a networking event? It would seem obvious that you would want to get to know as many people as you can. This means that the last thing you should do is stand by the food and look at your watch. You really need to mingle as much as possible.

I took a friend to a Business After Hours event years ago. He had his own small business and I was rooting for him to succeed. Shortly into the festivities I noticed he had disappeared, so I looked around for him. Sure enough he was alone in another part of the building. Later he admitted he was a wallflower and hated to talk to strangers. I felt like I was pushing a rope with him. As they say, you can lead a business owner to a networking event, but you can't make him mingle.

Remember that all of the other people in attendance are there for the same reason as you and that reason is to eventually get something out of it, and there is nothing wrong with that. Some will be there to reconnect with an old colleague, while others may just want to prospect.

Despite what you've heard, don't plan on handing out a stack of business cards with the expectation that your phone will ring off the hook the next day. That's a huge waste of your time and cards. I have a very specific game plan in mind each time I go to a networking event.

I carry a few business cards with me, but giving my card out is incidental. My goal is to *get* business cards from ten people. Also, I want to plant the seed for them to meet with me. Keep in mind that no one wants to be sold anything at a networking event because they are there to promote themselves.

When I meet someone for the first time, I introduce myself, get the other person's name, and ask some questions about their work. Then I might say something like, "I left my cards in the car. Can I get a business card from you so I can give you a call next week? Maybe we can set a time to talk more when it's a bit more appropriate." In other words, "We're all enjoying a beer right now but I do want to talk shop with you later."

Most often than not, I get a positive response. After my new acquaintance gives me her card, I'd say, "Thanks. I'll give you a call in the next few days to set a time to meet." Now she is expecting me to call and make the appointment. After I hit my goal of 10 cards, *then* I would reward myself by enjoying some food and spirits.

I had a sales manager who would always talk about making a "commitment objective" before anything you did at work. A "commitment objective" was nothing more than a goal you hope to accomplish in the next activity. If I was going to a networking meeting, my "CO" was to get 10 cards. When I went on an appointment, the CO might vary. Sometimes I would want to get some referrals, when other times my goal was to get a check. If you set a commitment objective before you walk in the door of a networking event or an appointment with a client, you will see some interesting results.

In a lot of ways, selling is like dating. You may want to close the deal on the first date, but more than likely you're going to have buy a few meals to earn some trust.

Consider this when you meet with your prospect. The best way to handle people in a meeting is to ask a lot of open ended questions. This will get them to open up and talk about themselves and their work. You would be amazed at how much you can gain from treating someone to a cup of coffee and just listening. Conversation starters such as, "Tell me about how you got started in business," or "Who is the best client for you?" can reap endless rewards. All of this leads us to the next part of this process.

Referrals

In any business, referrals are your best friend. These occur when one person likes you enough to tell their friends and associates about you. It's important to recognize the importance of this when receiving a referral because that lead could easily have gone to someone else, so now it's your responsibility to make sure you handle it as professionally as you possibly can. If you succeed, there is a great chance more will follow.

There are endless ways to get referrals and my best advice on this is to find one or two methods that work for you and stick with them.

I was taught the old school method of ending a meeting with a version of the following speech. "I make my living off of referrals. As a matter of fact, you were a referral, Mr. Johnson, so I would like you to give me some names of others I can help."

Typically, what was a great meeting would turn into a weird mental battle because deep down, that client or customer doesn't know you all that well. The last thing they want is to get a phone call from their annoyed friend. "Did you give my number to someone selling hanging baskets? I thought you liked me!"

In other words, people are reluctant to give referrals. Using a Jedi mind trick may work, but there are more subtle ways that can help you get leads.

If you are new to your industry, make sure the prospect knows this. Nice people will try to help you succeed, and may even consider you a "work in progress". The best line I ever used starting out was "If you were me and just starting in this business, who would be the first five people you would call?" Your customer will relate to what you are going through.

Your sweet little lady client will say to herself, "That poor bastard needs my help!"

Instead of asking for a referral, ask for an "introduction", which doesn't sound as scary. This method requires a bit of preparation, but can be very useful. Before you meet your prospect, do some research and find out who they know that you would like to meet.

In our example, your prospect, John, is a friend of Bill, who has a lot of money and hangs out at the yacht club. When you meet with John say something like, "Hey John, you know Bill, right? If he were to walk up right now you would introduce us to each other, correct? Well, since he's not here, could you introduce me to him through a phone call and tell him I'd like to introduce myself." Another rule of the universe is *People don't want to give referrals but they will introduce you to their friends.*

Another good line I use is "Just lie and say something nice about me."

Feed lists are a great way to find prospects. I've tried several methods of this, but generally, you want to have a list of names to "feed" your prospect to jog their referral memory bank. Let's suppose you are calling on an attorney, Stewart, a few days from now. You can either use the Yellow Pages or another reference source (Google "attorneys in my zip code") to find other attorneys in the same zip code. At the end of your appointment, pull out your list and ask vague questions about the other attorneys.

"Do you think I should call on Bob Thomas?" Stewart may tell you that Bob is a great guy or that Bob is a total jerk. If it's the former, ask if it's okay to mention your prospect when calling on good old Bob.

It won't feel like you're asking for a referral and they won't mind if you name drop. This way you can call on Bob and say, "I was talking with Stewart and he told me what a great guy you are."

Sometimes you'll hit the jackpot with a referral by having someone you least expect give you a treasure trove of good prospects. I'm not sure who first called it a "honey pot", but several of the guys in my office would always brag about it. "I wrote a policy for an old man and he gave me a 'honey pot' of referrals."

Remember to call your referrals in a timely manner. Amazingly, I know people who are reluctant to call someone who is actually expecting a call. If I'm expecting a call from you and you don't call for two weeks, I am going to think that you don't care about getting my business. Again, it sounds like dating, doesn't it?

Someone once said that referrals are like fish. If you don't do something with them quickly, they stink.

DUMB STORY

Business cards are one of those necessary evils in sales. They are most effective for drawings for door prizes and leaving behind with a tip when I go out to eat. An evil salesman I knew devised a sinister plan to combat bad service while sticking it to his competitor. Along with his own business cards, but carried a short stack of his competitor's cards as well.

If he received good service, he would leave a very generous tip with his business card on the table. He told me he would get a call from his server from time to time requesting his services.

But sometimes he would get bad service and when this happened, he'd leave a meager tip. Next to it, he would leave the card of his competitor. In his mind, he could hear the irate server going into the kitchen and complaining to the staff about that "cheap bastard who works for (fill in the blank)".

"You know that these people talk to each other and none of them will want to do business with that guy after that horrible tip he left," my co-worker would say with a giant smirk on his face.

With my parents and grandmother. I'm the short one looking away from the camera. I've always been a rebel.

Social Media

Everyone these days is on some kind of social media. Facebook, LinkedIn, Instagram, Twitter, and Snap Chat are just a few of the bigger platforms. And of course we can't forget the forgettable Google+. Despite what some social media "experts" say, the same rules apply here that apply to marketing in general. Not all platforms work for all industries. Facebook is primarily a way to keep in touch with friends and family. LinkedIn, on the other hand, is great for business networking. I still haven't figure out what Twitter is good for.

It was telling that on the day before Facebook took their company public, General Motors pulled all of their advertising on the site. Like I stated earlier, we have to account for our marketing dollars, and apparently there weren't enough people walking into GM dealerships because of promotions on Facebook.

Luckily for you, almost all of marketing you do can be *free*! Business pages on Facebook are a great way to get your message out to the masses. Some folks are using this in lieu of a website, while others, like myself, use it to direct traffic to my website. (www.SurfFinancialBrokers.com – Cheap plug!)

Another nice feature is you can invite your friends to see your posts, which can include industry tips, articles of interests or just about anything. I have seen pages that post funny photos that have absolutely nothing to do with their business get hundreds of "likes". On the other hand, there are times I've shared what I consider to be timely and important information, only to hear crickets chirping.

My friends, Chesty and Michele Chastain, of Chastain Media (www.chastainmedia.com) suggests the "big funnel" approach to online marketing. Have all of your pages linked to your website, thus funneling clients, customers, prospects and others to it. Did I mention they're social media geniuses?

I also like the idea of having links go back to those social media sites as well because I want to maximize the number of people who see me and my business.

Of late, I've been using an online tool called Buffer. Easy to setup, you can put all of your social media sites under one roof, so to speak, and post to some or all of them at once. If I see an article that I think will interest people, I can share it on Buffer, which in turn shares it to my Facebook page, along with my LinkedIn, Twitter and, yes, even my sad Google+ pages. Also, Buffer allows you to schedule your posts so that they aren't flooding someone's feed all at once or when your prospects are sleeping.

As I mentioned earlier, most of this can be done for free, and it can be tricky to find out what your rate of return is. Your time is money, so remember to factor in the amount of time you spend on social media. I personally don't spend more than 20 minutes each day working on social media because I've gotten mixed results at best and I can probably use that time wisely elsewhere.

By far, the most productive of all of the platforms for my business has been LinkedIn. Designed for business networking, LinkedIn isn't the place to post pictures of your kids or political rants. Instead, it can give you a great way to find people (called "Connections") you would like to have as clients, employees, business associates, etc.

After making a connection, I have been able to meet these people in person by sending a short note of introduction like this.

Thanks for being a "connection" on LinkedIn. I would like an opportunity to meet with you in the next week or so to introduce myself and to learn more about your work. If you have 10-15 minutes available, please call me at ...

This is a very non-threatening kind of note. No one wants to be "sold" on LinkedIn, but they are willing to meet with you in a public place, have a cup of coffee (again, make it your treat), and tell you about their business. Verbiage is its own reward, and getting someone to open up to you means they already trust you.

I may send out 10 or more of these a week when I have nothing scheduled. My results surprised even me, because I have had about a 10% success rate of getting an appointment doing this. That's not bad when you consider that I didn't have to ask for a referral or cold call.

Something else interesting happened as well. I found that I could use similar language in a message to other insurance agents in my area, as well as across the country. Through networking with other agents I have also learned some valuable sales tips.

I've also been able to recruit a few agents as well by using LinkedIn to set "phone appointments". So not only am I getting a few clients but I'm creating another revenue stream by bringing more agents into the fold.

In general, I highly suggest LinkedIn as a tool for you. Their "groups" are specific to many industries or geographical areas. Again, more opportunities to meet people. I'm always surprised at the number of business professionals who don't want to sign up for LinkedIn because they "don't have the time", but they will spend hours on Facebook looking at cat videos.

One thing that always perplexes me is people who take the time to complete a LinkedIn profile and don't really want to network, but will complain they don't get any business out of it.

Considering how many "followers" I have on Twitter, it has been one of the most counterproductive endeavors ever. At the time of this writing, I have over 12,000 followers and not one of them is a client. Even though I still post on Twitter through Buffer, I don't really take the time to worry about it. I'm sure it works for some people in other industries, but my ROI is probably negative.

Google+ was supposed to be the next Facebook, but anyone that uses it will understand why it has not succeeded. People post the same content that is on their other social media pages. From realtors to news site, the same information is on their other feeds.

Sometimes I mention Google+ just to get a reaction. Most people comment on how boring it is or they just don't care for the layout. I seriously hope that the smart people at Google can figure out how to make the site more attractive.

You work hard, you play hard.

Blogs and Podcasts

Many people insist on Blogging, which is writing a short article on a subject in hopes of getting subscribers. Ultimately, you want people to think of you as the expert in your area, and blogging supposedly gives you a way to accomplish this.

Are you really good at pottery? Then you can write a blog each week with tips about "throwing clay". Do you want to let people know about your fundraising work? Blog about that.

As you blog, you will want to build an audience of subscribers. Remember that you are a small fish in a giant ocean because there are literally millions of other blogs. One way to get people to take notice of yours is to link it to your other feeds.

YouTube is great way of making a video blog if you feel comfortable enough to have people watch you speak. You can record and upload a talk on any subject and it will be archived, which is great if you want to send your prospect a link at a later date.

Do yourself a favor and have a very honest friend watch your blog before you upload it. I'm not saying you're unattractive, but maybe you have a face for podcasts.

Podcasts are like a radio broadcast version of a blog. You can interview guests, opine about the state of your industry and let everyone know how smart you are. The difference is that the audience will now hear your voice and the tone you are using, so sarcasm sounds like sarcasm.

Anyone can start a podcast with some recording software and microphone. I thoroughly enjoy listening to podcasts on a variety of subjects. I was even interviewed by Mike Oglesbee of www.maximizedmind.com, on his podcast. Hopefully, he didn't lose subscribers after that one.

Before jumping into podcasting, I would advise you to listen to a few first to get an idea of how you want to present yourself to the public. Theme music is a nice touch, but most of all, enthusiasm in your voice is the key.

Paying for Leads

Buying leads is a way to get around the pain and agony of not wanting to prospect (see Chapter 6, The World's Best Pickup Line). Surely someone has fared well this way, but unfortunately, I haven't heard a lot of success stories when it comes to buying leads.

One insurance agent I worked with told me he spent $250 on a lead service. He could choose three Zip codes to get leads from. The names were to come to him via email and he had to respond quickly because other agents who had chosen those Zip codes got the same leads.

He would get a notification email early in the morning and try to be the first to contact the lead. None of the prospects wanted to spend a lot of money and he felt that many weren't seriously shopping for insurance to begin with. The agent concluded that these "leads" were insufferable insomniacs and, out of boredom, decided to surf the net looking for life insurance in the wee hours. In other words, they were kicking the tires. When these people entered their email address to get the "free quote" the system automatically notified several agents.

I do know of real estate agents that use a system similar to this and it has more than paid for itself. It really depends on the industry you sell in and the quality of the leads.

I have known agents who bought leads only to find out that no one took the time to verify the list. The names literally came out of the phone book or worse, a cemetery.

Side note: Try to do business with people who do business with you. It just makes sense. If someone is going to spend their money with you, shouldn't you return the favor?

This is why I keep my trips to Wal-Mart to a minimum. Wal-Mart isn't going to give me any business so why should I waste my time spending money with them? The odds of you getting your foot in the door of a major retailer or manufacturer are slim, unless you have a cousin whose best friend is the sister of a buyer for the company.

On the other hand, I have a client who owns a high end bakery. When I need to buy a cake I will give them my business even though it may be a little bit more expensive. It's a great way of saying thank you and ensuring referrals.

There will be times when you can't do business with a client or customer. That's okay, but the least you can do is give them an awesome referral whichl could blossom into more business for them. And remind your client you sent them that referral.

Are you buying leads from here?

Chapter 9

HOW TO BE A GREAT CUSTOMER

"The customer is not always right, but you have to let him think he is." - Fred Kane, self-described "average salesman"

"The customer is always right!" Not hardly. If anyone tells you otherwise, they aren't your friend so stay away from them.

My years as a retail manager taught me to treat sales people correctly. Can you imagine shopping at 10am drunk and belligerent? It happens more than you think. Do you let your kids run loose in department stores? Have you dropped off your pre-teen kids at the mall on a Friday night? Oh yes, it happens. As employees it sucked for us because we didn't sign on to be your baby sitter and neither did those mall security guards.

I get it. You want, or should I say, expect to be treated fairly. We all do. As a friend of mine says all the time we he receives below average customer service, "Who's paying who around here?" But believe me when I tell you that not everyone is trying to scam you or rip you off.

The following is a short list of things that you can do to make your customer experience better.

Don't be a PITA (pain in the ass). This shouldn't have to be explained. It's common knowledge and something you should have learned in grade school.

We once had a lady come in to the store with a sales receipt from another store located across the state line and she was returning an inexpensive item. Because of the difference in the state sales tax there was a three cent difference between her receipt and our cash register. With her small child looking on, she decided to make an example of me and my high school aged employee by screaming that she should get the full refund. My sales clerk, hungover from the previous evening's festivities, let her rant for a minute. Then he reached into his pocket, pulling out a nickel. He slowly placed in on the counter, put his index finger on it and angrily slid it in her direction.

"Keep the change," he sneered. This made her even more upset, but she got what she deserved. She made some comment under her breath about never coming back.

My employee looked at me and said, "If she had hung in there I would have given that bitch a dollar just to make her go away."

She was a PITA.

Do what you say you're going to do. When starting a business, a sales career or any other kind of new venture, customers are the lifeblood. It is very frustrating when I meet someone for the first time and they ask what I do. When I tell them they say, "Give me your card. I definitely need to talk to you!" It's as if they genuinely want me to help them.

But they never call back. Ever. Don't ask me why people do this, but it happens more than you would think. Maybe they're trying to be nice, but it's not nice. So now I ask for their number and let them know that if I don't hear from them in a couple of weeks, I will call. If there is any hesitation on their part, I quickly know if they "really needed to talk to you."

Respect business hours. Nobody wants to work all day long. With that in mind, if someone has a valid emergency or just needs a question answered, I will usually do my best to accommodate. You want people to respect your work hours and you should do the same for others.

When I managed a store in the mall, there was a 10-screen Cineplex across the hall that always seemed to have a movie finish five minutes before our closing time. My store would suddenly get extremely busy when my crew and I were ready to shut down the place. We would flick the lights and lower the front gate a bit to drop hints for people that we were ready to leave, even though they just arrived. Was this wrong? Absolutely not! Those people had all day to come in and browse. Waiting until we were closing to shop was rude.

Failure to plan on your part does not constitute an emergency on my part. I'm not sure who came up with that phrase but it's accurate. When it comes to insurance policies that require some sort of health underwriting, such as a health or disability policy, some people will put it off until it's just too late.

A friend of mine came to my home unannounced one evening to buy life insurance. It was very unusual that he did this and as he left he mentioned that he was going to the hospital. At this point it was around 9pm and I told him visiting hours were probably over. He replied that he wasn't going to visit anyone, but was on his way to the emergency room to get checked out for severe pain. As he pulled out of my driveway I put his application for life insurance in the shredder. This policy wouldn't be issued and I wasn't about to waste other people's time like he had just wasted mine.

DUMB STORY

One of the jobs of a sales manager is to ride along with a member of the sales crew to make sure they are doing their job correctly. On one occasion my manager, Tom, rode along with me . Tom and I found an old wooden house on the side of the road in the middle of nowhere. We had to walk on rotted boards to get across giant mud puddles just to reach the front porch. We knocked on the door and a young man in his 20's answered. He was very happy to see us, which struck me as odd. Enthusiastically inviting us in, he gave us a place to sit on the couch and said, "Show me what you got!"

I started into my presentation and noticed that there were several nicely dressed ladies walking back and forth across the room. "What are they doing?" I asked.

"My mother just passed away. They're getting dressed for the funeral."

I looked at Tom and he looked back at me. I said, "If you need to get ready for your mom's funeral, we can come back another time."

"Nah, it's cool. Now show me what you got," he said as his sisters walked from room to room.

Something wasn't quite right but it's not every day that you get a willing audience, so I jumped back into my sales presentation. Tom sat quietly and watched me work my magic until our prospect looked at him and jumped up.

"Man, you look bored. I got something for you!" He reached under the cushions of the worn out chair he was sitting in and pulled out three old magazines. They were folded over as if they had been used to swat mosquitos. Tom opened them and his eyes grew as wide as saucers.

Tom was holding some of the dirtiest porn magazines I've ever seen. Definitely not the kind you see behind the counter at the convenience store. This kid looked at Tom and nodded. "You look at those while he keeps talking."

I grinned at Tom and said, "If you see something you haven't seen before, just shoot it."

That's when we realized that this was one crazy bastard. His mother had just died, his sisters were preparing for the funeral and he was insisting that I finish my sales pitch while my manager browsed through our client's porn collection. I hurried to complete my talk as I could see Tom squirming uncomfortably in his seat.

Closing, I pulled out a pen and acted as if I was going to fill out the application. "How would you like to pay for this?" I asked.

"Oh, I don't want to buy anything. But you can keep those magazines," he insisted.

"I'm good," I said, "but Tom would love one." Tom grimaced as our host insisted that we take all of them.

We got the hell out of there as fast as we could. I tossed the periodicals in the back seat of Tom's car with every intention of leaving them there. He looked at me like he had never seen a crazy person before.

"What the hell was that about?"

"I think he had a screw loose. At least you got some reading material out of it." I smiled.

"Screw you! I have a girlfriend and she is not going to see those magazines. Take them with you."

I agreed but secretly hid one under a floor mat in his car. I wonder who found it first, Tom or his girlfriend.

I have never been in a sales meeting that actually looked like this, but...

...this looks familiar!

Chapter 10

EVERYONE WANTS APPROVAL

"The world is full of incompetence...which of course applies to everyone's job, not just sales!!"
Gale Mulcahy - Advertising sales professional

There is a lot of psychology involved in selling. People can be naturally resistant when someone approaches them in a "salesy" way. I can't stand the people who work at a kiosk in a mall or strip center and call you over like panhandlers. But as a people watcher, I enjoy looking on as shoppers, who earlier were in a "buying mood", do their best to avoid eye contact and elude these sales people.

But I digress. We, as sales professionals, need to make our jobs as easy as possible and find the path of least resistance. The best way to do this is to get into the head of our prospect and find out which buttons to push, as well as knowing when to push them.

One of these buttons is *validation*. Humans always seek validation, no matter if it's in our personal, professional or financial lives. We want people to like our choices.

Remember the last time you bought a car? You showed it off and you loved it when people told you how nice it was. You *needed* to hear how great your choice was.

Or think back to the first time you introduced your significant other to your friends. "She's cute!" or "He seems like a very nice guy!" makes us feel good.

On the other hand, no one wants to hear how bad of a choice they made. "You spent way too much money on that car! Are you nuts?" Now that I feel like an idiot, punch me in the gut while you're at it.

So the bottom line is that when we purchase anything, on some level in our brain, we consider what others will think of that purchase, as well as questioning our own judgement. Which leads me to my favorite law of sales: ***People buy on the approval of others.***

If I know you have great respect for George Stein, I might let you know that good old George just bought something from me. If it's good enough for George, it's good enough for you, right? Smelling blood in the water, I ask if you are paying with cash or a check.

Take a second to think of all this ways you can use this to your advantage. Discreetly dropping the name of someone who is influential in your community can help open some doors for you. I've been known to name drop.

"I'm sorry I'm running late, but I had a hard time with the traffic near Joe Tyler's business."

Of course, you should always ask if it's okay before dropping someone's name. Some people want (or expect) confidentiality when doing business with you. But others will have no problem with you mentioning them to a prospect.

"Bob, you are a well-respected lawyer. Is it okay if I mention you if I meet another attorney?" Make it Bob's choice as to whether or not he will allow you to use his name.

Don't try to be sneaky. People will begin to think of you as dishonest. Also, privacy laws may prohibit you from giving names of your customers depending on your industry.

You can be vague sometimes. If I'm giving a talk to a group I may say something like, "I just met a doctor who wanted to know where he could put $20,000 each year without tax consequences." Did it happen? Yes. Do I have to disclose the name of the doctor? Not really. People generally think doctors are smart.

Compliment people after they buy to let them know they chose their purchase wisely. If they truly respect and trust you, your comments can make them feel much better about their purchase.

Sincerity is the key. If you say, "I think you chose well," with a smug look on your face, you'll come across as a jerk. I once dealt with an exterminator who grinned the entire time he explained the infestation in my home.

An excellent way to get the approval of others is through endorsements. When I can get someone to write a couple of sentences on my behalf, I can use it on my website and other brochures. If you have a business page on social media, I highly recommend you ask your best clients to give you a quick recommendation. Don't forget to offer to return the favor.

Try to get an endorsement from someone likable and that people know. You'll be defeating the purpose with an endorsement by the village idiot or a hermit that has no sphere of influence.

A good way to get an endorsement is to give one. Pick a week to give ten unsolicited endorsements each day. The easiest method is to use LinkedIn. Assuming you have plenty of "connections", you can find one profile, write a short blurb (a couple of sentences) and copy and paste it to others profiles. One of the features of LinkedIn that I like, and that you should be aware of, is that people are notified when someone looks at their profile. When they get a notification that you've left an endorsement they may send you a thank you note and sometimes an "return endorsement" for you!

Because we value the approval of others, this rule is often true in many aspects of our lives. For example, a hiring manager, who in essence is making an investment in a new staff member, will requests references. If a prospective employee doesn't work out, the employer can always say, "Well, I checked her references and they said she was a super employee." Of course, we all know to give references who will speak highly of us.

Like I mentioned earlier, we are truly selling

ourselves. As such, we need approval from our peers and the peers of our buyers. The obvious way of doing this is to make sure you have a good rapport with your community and your clients.

Your reputation is like your credit score. If yours is good, you can have whatever you want. A wise man once told me the key to success was to be honest with people and offer a fair price. If you do just those two things, you don't have to worry about your reputation.

At the tender age of 19. The hairstyle was criminal.

DUMB STORY

Back in my door-to-door selling days, our sales crew would work one county at a time. We were provided with a list of people in that county who already had a policy with us, and we were expected to write their names on cards. During the presentation, we would pull out the "power names" and read them aloud in hopes of having the prospect recognize one or two. With all of the privacy laws in force today, I'm not sure if you could get away with this anymore.

As I would flip through the cards, I would

mention the names. "As you can see, Mr. Emmitt Johnson from the gas station has a policy with us, as well as Mary Stone." If I was lucky, my prospect would pipe up.

"I know Mary Stone. She plays the organ at our church. Such a sweet lady!" Jackpot!

The majority of time, though, this didn't work. Many prospective customers just didn't know the names on the cards. We realized that we needed someone's name who had a much higher profile.

We were working a rural county in eastern North Carolina and each morning we would meet at a local diner or breakfast joint to discuss any issues from the day before. Then we would give our sales numbers to our manager. He would want to know how many policies we had sold the day earlier. Typically, it would sound like this.

"Chris, how many?"

"Three," I would say.

"Bob, how many?"

Bob would answer, "Four."

There were a lot of twos, threes, fours, and the occasional five. So it was surprising when a fellow named Tim calmly said, "Eight." He must have just gotten lucky, we thought.

But the next day, we gave our numbers again, and Tim had another eight in the bag. What the hell? Tim was making us look bad. We wanted to find out his secret?

After the meeting, a couple of us cornered Tim. "What are you doing differently?" we asked. Tim laughed. He was just like us. Right out of college, sarcastic and not giving a crap about a career in door-to-door insurance sales.

"You know those power names? I added one that isn't on the list they gave us." I wasn't sure this was allowed.

Apparently a local high profile Klansman lived in that county. He had been in the headlines for years and most of us thought the guy was probably in jail for his activities. Tim wrote the guy's name on a card and used it during his presentation for shits and giggles, pretending to be oblivious as to the Klansman's history. He said, "Believe it or not, these people love this guy. He's like a folk legend in these parts."

So, a few of us tried it out and put the Klansman's name on a card. Did he have a policy with us? I don't think so, and it really didn't matter. At this point, this was no longer a matter of compliance to the rules, but more of a study in sociology.

The next day, sales figures went like this.

"Tim, how many?"

"Seven," Tim answered.

"Chris, how many?"

"Eight!" I proudly replied.

"Nick, how many?"

Nick answered, "Seven!"

The trend continued and our manager started to suspect something was up, besides our sales numbers. He heard our chuckling and shook his head. "Do I even want to know what is going on here or should I just say 'thank you' and keep my mouth shut?"

"It's probably best not to ask too many questions," someone answered.

The following few weeks in that county continued in that vein. And when we were moved to another county, a couple of guys spent some time trying to discreetly find out who the local prominent Klansman, or equivalent racist, in the area was. It never really panned out and we dropped the matter when people started to think we were asking questions in hopes of joining a Neo-Nazi group. But for a few weeks, we found success through a very warped "approval buying" method.

Chapter 11

THE EVER LOVING PERSISTENCE

"I design, manufacture, distribute, and sell elevator buttons. I specialize in the fourth floor. And I don't mean to brag, but I'm such a good salesman that I could sell one of my fourth-floor elevator buttons to the owner of a three-story building." - Jarod Kintz, Author

"Persistency" has a few meanings in this business. "Sales persistency" is important for those of us who sell someone a "monthly bill", like an insurance policy or a phone system. We rely on someone buying from us and *continuing* to make payments because we get a small residual commission that can potentially keep paying for many years.

Of course, being persistent is a hallmark of great salespeople. Hanging in there when people say they aren't interested is part of the work. When someone says that "now isn't a good time", I ask if I can keep in touch. If they say yes, I put their name in a "tickler" file, which reminds me to check in on them in a few months.

If your prospect is expecting you to call, do so. It only takes a minute and can lead to big sales. Years ago I met a middle-aged confirmed bachelor at a networking meeting. We chatted and it didn't take long to realize he really didn't have a need for my insurance products.

However, a year later things changed. By calling him and asking "How are things going?" I learned that a recent death in his family left him caring for an adult special needs family member. Suddenly he did need some life insurance! My persistence paid off.

The other great method of checking in with a prospect is by "dripping" on them. Yep, it sounds disgusting, but it isn't. Like Chinese water torture without the torture part, "dripping" is a low-key way to let the client know you haven't forgotten about them.

One way to succeed at this is to send them an article pertaining to their profession once a month through email. Attach a note saying, "Saw this and thought it might be of interest to you." Or you can congratulate them for an award or wish them a Happy Birthday. The goal of all this is to keep you in the prospect's mind.

Ask your client if you can subscribe them to your monthly newsletter. You can produce this yourself or have a service do it for you. Make sure an up to date photo of you is included, but more importantly, ensure that the information provided is something of use to your prospect.

By constantly keeping in contact by dripping instead of being pushy and too aggressive, you may eventually get that sale. I've even had clients thank me for not giving up on them.

Another meaning of persistency pertains to how long we, as salespeople, continue to work for a particular company. The life insurance business, for instance, has an extremely low persistency rate. Some estimate that less than 10% of agents are still around after three years.

According to Dusty Baker on his website, MyAgentAdvice.com, "Statistics show that 80% of new real estate agents don't make it to their one year anniversary. This incredibly high attrition rate proves that discouragement and disappointment are rampant in the real estate industry."

Unfortunately, this is the norm for most sales positions, especially those that are paid solely by commission. Many people are hired, but few last more than a few months before they are disillusioned by the long hours, rejection and lack of support. A former co-worker of mine used to say that salespeople rarely get fired because "they quit way before it comes to that".

One company I worked for was famous for hiring everyone that could get through a background check. Then they would train them on the products for a few days and send them out in the field. Referred to as "throwing them at the wall and see who sticks", it didn't take long for the rest of the sales team to make wagers on who would last. The longest. Bitter, the agent would inevitably leave. And adding insult to injury, a few would still owe the company money for commissions that had been advanced.

Needless to say, a lot of this could have been avoided if the hiring agent or recruiter had been upfront and honest during the interview instead of bullshitting a recruit and telling them what they wanted to hear. Letting someone know that the job is hard, lonely and filled with rejection should be part of the process.

Personally, I have always thought that since there are "truth in advertising" laws, there should also be "truth in hiring" laws. Ultimately it would save people time and energy if someone would just be upfront and honest with them.

But instead of honesty, a prospective sales rep with no experience will hear "You have a great personality and I think you're going to be great at this!" Thus the name of this book. I'm sure someone will cite an exception to the rule, but even in my own practice I try to be as honest as possible with people. It just doesn't make sense to invest a lot of time training someone who isn't going to be there in a few months .

Because of this almost all of my agents must have a few years of experience in the industry before I even consider them. And my most successful agents don't need me to hold a "rah rah session" to get motivated, because they already *are* motivated.

Epilogue

Not every client is a whale, but the world is full of potential whales. Good examples of potential whales are grad students, startups and trust fund babies (maybe that last one is a bit too early). Building a relationship with these people early in the game can pay off in spades in the long run. And you will always have your "I helped her before she made her millions" story. Look for the diamond in the rough.

Sarah Bernhardt as Theodora

A great example is Empress Theodora. The daughter of an animal trainer in ancient Rome, (her father died when she was a young child), she soon became an actress and a prostitute, known for her "acrobatic skills". Upon leaving the "entertainment" industry, she caught the eye of a Roman soldier, Justinian.. As the woman behind the man, she helped her future husband's rise to emperor, and she became the empress, and later, a saint.

There are a couple of conclusions to be made from this. First and foremost, we can see that relationship selling definitely works! Secondly, one good customer can reap a lifetime of fortune.

So are you up to the task? Even though I've probably never spoken to you, I think you're going to be great at this!

ABOUT THE AUTHOR

Chris Castanes began his career in insurance after graduating from North Carolina State University in 1985 and in 1989, he moved to North Myrtle Beach, SC, where he resides with his wife, Amy and daughter, Elena.

Chris is the president of Surf Financial Brokers, located in North Myrtle Beach, SC.